A GUIDE
TO THE NATURE CONSERVANCY'S
PRESERVES IN WASHINGTON

By David George Gordon

Photography by Keith Lazelle

The
Nature
Conservancy®

Author ....................................................David George Gordon

Photography ....................................................Keith Lazelle

Cover and Book Design ....................................................Sandy Wing

Illustration ....................................................Joyce Berger

Cover Lettering Design ....................................Tim Girvin Design, Inc

Editor ....................................................Gordon Todd

Additional Photography:
Jeffrey S. Boucher, Gary Braasch, Russ Jolley, Stephen J. Krasemann
Rich Landers, Harold E. Malde, Kevin Morris, Charles Nishida,
Michael Parker, Joel Rogers, Bonnie Lee Sharpe, Mark Sheehan,
Barb Taubman, Gordon Todd, Sunny Walter, Art Wolfe

Editorial Assistance ..........................Rachel Bard, Mary Louise Conte

Photo Assistance ............................................................Kevin Sink

Technical Assistance:
Georgia Gellert, Sarah Greene, Martha McKee, Victor Scheffer,
Zachary Semke, Nature Conservancy staff

Research ....................................................Linda Lewis

Color Separations and Prepress Services ......................Wy'east Color

Printing ............................................................The Boeing Company

Published by The Nature Conservancy
Washington Chapter
217 Pine Street, Suite 1100
Seattle, WA 98101

Manufactured in the United States of America

Library of Congress Catalog Card Number 92-085124

Library of Congress information available

ISBN 0-89886-350-3

*Front cover photo: Skagit River Bald
Eagle Natural Area by Keith Lazelle.* **Back
cover photos:** *Yellow Island Preserve,
great blue herons at Bone River Estuary,
common blue at Dishman Hills Preserve by
Keith Lazelle; bird watchers at Foulweather
Bluff Preserve by Gordon Todd.*

Distributed by The Mountaineers Books
1011 SW Klickitat Way, Suite 107, Seattle, WA 98134
1-800-553-4453; FAX 206-223-6306

*Printed on Recycled Paper*

*"The first rule of
intelligent tinkering is
to save all the parts."*

—Aldo Leopold

*The Nature Conservancy
is a private, non-profit
organization dedicated to
preserving plants, animals
and natural communities
that represent the
diversity of life on Earth
by protecting the lands and
waters they need to survive.
To date the Conservancy
and its members have
protected more than
6.3 million acres in the
United States and Canada,
often through direct
purchase of ecologically
significant lands.
The Conservancy currently
owns more than 1,300
preserves, the largest
system of private nature
sanctuaries in the world.*

## ACKNOWLEDGMENTS

Thanks to the generosity and encouragement of the Boeing Company, The Nature Conservancy is able to put this guide to the preserves of Washington in your hands. Donation of printing services for this book is an example of Boeing's outstanding and long-term corporate support of The Nature Conservancy in Washington.

Production of this book was also supported by the generous financial contributions of the Puget Sound Fund and the Weyerhaeuser Company Foundation, both leading long-time supporters of the Conservancy's Washington Chapter.

# TABLE OF CONTENTS

*Bowl-shaped grass widow flowers burst from the ground each spring. Members of the iris family, they grow in grassy areas in Washington.*
*(Keith Lazelle)*

*Once common in the lowlands of the Pacific Northwest, the state-threatened western pond turtle still survives on the banks of a handful of Washington waterways.*

# FOREWORD

# THE NATURE CONSERVANCY IN WASHINGTON STATE

*"Once a species is lost, it will take a new sun, a new moon and a new dawn of creation before it can be replaced."*

—William Beebe

Each winter in Western Washington, hundreds of bald eagles from across the Northwest, Alaska and Canada congregate in the conifers and cottonwoods and on the gravel bars of the swift-flowing Skagit River. Less than a month before the eagles' appearance, the river is occupied by other seasonal life forms—thousands of adult chum salmon, returning after several years in the open ocean to the fresh-water tributaries of their birth. Mouths agape after the long, hard upstream journey, their dull crimson bodies battered and torn, the fish expend their last shreds of energy to pair off and spawn in the Skagit's shallows. Having done their part to ensure the continued survival of their species, the spawned-out chum soon perish, littering the banks and bars with their rotting remains.

Opportunistic feeders, the bald eagles are quick to capitalize on this ready source of protein. With an audible flapping of their massive wings, both adults and adolescents swoop down to the river's edge, tearing at the decayed flesh with sharp talons and beaks. Occasional squabbles erupt over ownership of the chum, with young eagles snatching food from the mouths of their elders.

As dusk approaches, the birds abandon the banks of the Skagit, soar high above the river and glide in great arcs toward their communal night roosts a short distance inland. Here, they will wait out the darkness, sheltered from wind and snowfall among the tall trees. With the first light of dawn, they will resume their feasting on salmon remains.

Between December and February, the bald eagles replay these scenes each day, as have their ancestors for countless generations. But in the 19th and 20th centuries, increased human activity threatened to upset the seasonal cycles of both salmon and eagles. Throughout the Northwest, the steady encroachment of agriculture, forestry, industry and development has taken its toll on the Skagit's natural habitats and inhabitants. The bald eagle is listed as a threatened species in Washington state and an endangered species in 43 other states.

To counter this persistent development and protect the bald eagle, the Washington Chapter of The Nature Conservancy bought its first parcels of land along the Skagit in 1976. Since then, others have joined the Conservancy in protecting this critical habitat for our national symbol. By 1992, the total area of this important stronghold, the Skagit River Bald Eagle Natural Area, had grown from 875 acres to more than 4,500 acres.

*Bald eagles return each winter to the Conservancy's Skagit River preserve.*
*(Keith Lazelle)*

*Several species of Indian paintbrush thrive within the Conservancy's preserves. They are believed to be partially parasitic, requiring the presence of certain host plants to survive.*
(Keith Lazelle)

# THE VALUE OF BIODIVERSITY

From its inception, The Nature Conservancy's Washington Chapter has focused its energies and resources on buying and managing nature preserves like the Skagit River Bald Eagle Natural Area. This straightforward focus on habitat has worked well to protect the "lifeboats" of plant and animal diversity—or biodiversity—that would otherwise have vanished from our landscape.

While there are many reasons why we should protect the Earth's species and ecosystems, one of the most compelling to some is self-interest. The natural world provides our economic foundation with countless medical, agricultural and commercial products. "The living things of this earth are our resources and life support systems," wrote Elliot Norse. "Every bite of food you eat comes from living things. Every sip of water you drink has been cleansed by living things. The oxygen in your every breath comes from living things. Humankind is utterly dependent on biological diversity."

In the Northwest, the Pacific yew tree is a good example. Previously overlooked and unwittingly destroyed during timber harvest, the yew is now widely recognized for its medicinal value. Contained in the bark of the yew is a substance known as taxol, which has proven to be an effective drug in the treatment of certain types of cancer. Had we driven the yew to extinction, this cancer drug would never have been discovered.

*Conservancy scientists conduct field studies to identify potential preserves.*
(Jeffrey S. Boucher)

But as species vanish, so do their potential advantages to the human race. The natural rate of extinction was one species every thousand years. The impacts of modern humans have dramatically increased this rate. Current estimates tell us the world is losing three or more species every day.

At this alarming rate, scientists fear that the planet's intricate web of life is unraveling. Nature and all its creatures—including people—are one complex, interrelated organism. A few destroyed parts, or extinctions, may not be noticed. But as more and more plants and animals disappear, the system faces the likelihood of coming apart.

"Ecosystems, like well-made airplanes, tend to have redundant subsystems and other design features that permit them to continue functioning after absorbing a certain amount of abuse," wrote biologists Paul and Anne Ehrlich in *Extinction: The Causes and Consequences of the Disappearance of Species*. "A dozen rivets, or a dozen species, might never be missed. On the other hand, a 13th rivet popped from a wing flap, or the extinction of a key species ... could lead to a serious accident."

There are also important aesthetic and ethical reasons for saving species. As E. O. Wilson and Paul Ehrlich recently wrote, "Because *Homo sapiens* is the dominant species on Earth, we and many others think that people have an absolute moral responsibility to protect what are our only known living companions in the universe. ... The popularity of ecotourism, bird watching, wildlife films, pet-keeping and gardening attest that human beings gain great aesthetic rewards from those companions."

These and many other compelling reasons are why The Nature Conservancy does its work.

Throughout the Conservancy's history, concerned citizens from all walks of life have come together to assist in the protection of bio-diversity. And while the Conservancy's work is directed by science, it is the inspiration and dedication of people that transform the organization's goals into realities.

"One of the most exciting aspects of The Nature Conservancy's direct conservation approach is that one person can truly make a difference," said Elliot Marks, Washington director of the Conservancy. "One person with a dream to save a special piece of land can often make it happen. And that's what I think this organization in large part is about: Caring people doing something very tangible to make the Earth a better place for future generations."

*One of the largest birds in North America, the endangered American white pelican is exceptionally wary of people. It nests on isolated islands and gravel bars, cloistered away from human disturbance.*
(Sunny Walter)

The Conservancy traces its roots back to 1917, when members of the Ecological Society of America met to address one major concern—the loss of natural lands in the United States. Following this meeting, Ecological Society members established a pair of work groups, the Committee for the Preservation of Natural Conditions and the Committee for the Study of Plant and Animal Communities. In 1946, the members of both committees formed the Ecologists Union. Four years later, the Ecologists Union changed its name to The Nature Conservancy, which in 1951 was incorporated as a non-profit organization devoted to science and public education.

## A SCIENTIFIC FOUNDATION

Based on a solid foundation of natural science, The Nature Conservancy uses a three-pronged conservation strategy that involves:

- IDENTIFYING the species and ecosystems in greatest need of immediate protection and the specific geographic areas that can best ensure their survival.
- PROTECTING habitats and natural systems through direct land acquisition by gift or purchase, and by assisting government and other conservation organizations in similar land acquisition efforts.
- MANAGING lands for the long-term protection of species and ecosystems using staff and volunteer land stewards; supporting scientific research on the needs of the rare species and ecosystems.

*The Bone River Estuary, one of two preserves in southwest Washington's Willapa Bay watershed co-owned by the Conservancy and the state, encompasses nearly 1,700 acres of high-quality marsh and forest habitats.*
(Michael Parker)

## THE WASHINGTON CHAPTER IS BORN

The move to charter a Nature Conservancy chapter in Washington was spearheaded by Charles Wesley Bovee—the first mayor of Bellevue, Washington—when he brought together a few people in his living room on August 20, 1958. The following year, a core group of members decided to compile an inventory of selected natural areas in need of preservation. Ira Philip Lloyd, a woodworker from Bothell, and Arthur R. Kruckeberg, a University of Washington botanist, agreed to chair the "State of Washington Nature Conservancy Survey Committee." In 1960, a charter was granted to establish a Washington chapter.

An important period of research and growth followed. The first in a series of field trips was initiated to evaluate natural areas as potential preserve sites. Members of the Washington Chapter explored Carlisle Bog near Copalis, Eagle Cliffs on Cypress Island, Swan Creek in Tacoma and the Mima Mounds—all of which have since been protected as parks or preserves. Wildflower Acres became the first area acquired by the Washington Chapter, which later transferred title to the 25-acre preserve, along with responsibility for its management, to Western Washington University.

In 1966, the Conservancy chartered an Inland Empire Chapter. The movement to form this Eastern Washington chapter, which also encompassed portions of northern Idaho, was led by George E. Hudson, professor of zoology at Washington State University and an active Conservancy member since 1959.

Soon, a united Washington Chapter was formed, and in 1972 the Conservancy opened its first Northwest office for Washington, Oregon, Idaho, Montana, Wyoming and Alaska.

*Moxee Bog Preserve's rare insect treasure, the silver-bordered bog fritillary, rests on an invasive alien plant, the Canadian thistle.*
*(Barb Taubman)*

*The western grey squirrel once occurred throughout Washington's oak-conifer woodlands, but is now threatened in the state. The Conservancy is working to protect habitat for this furry native.*

As the Conservancy's efforts, membership and successes continued to multiply, a Washington Chapter office was opened in 1979 to bring professional, full-time focus to the preservation of natural areas throughout the state.

The next few years were characterized by steady growth and increased preserve acquisitions. During this period, the Washington Chapter also forged important links with private and government agencies responsible for managing environmentally sensitive areas.

## A COOPERATIVE APPROACH TO CONSERVATION

Today, in addition to its own preserve acquisition efforts, the Washington Chapter assists federal and state agencies, individuals and private organizations to ensure that key areas representing the state's legacy of native grasslands, wetlands, islands and forests are retained. In a spirit of cooperation and drawing on the shared pool of scientific information, the Washington Chapter has successfully assisted state agencies in the development of comprehensive strategies and new funding for saving vanishing species and natural systems.

In 1972, the Washington State Legislature enacted the Natural Area Preserves Act establishing a statewide system of Natural Area Preserves (NAP). Then in 1977, the Washington Chapter of the Conservancy, the state Department of Natural Resources and the Department of Game (now the Department of Wildlife) created the

Washington Natural Heritage Program—the state's only data bank of native species and ecosystems. The Conservancy funded the Heritage Program until 1982, when it was transferred into state government.

Among the Heritage Program's important contributions is the biennial state Natural Heritage Plan, a blueprint for natural area protection in Washington.

Under this program, the Commissioner of Public Lands appoints a 15-member Natural Heritage Advisory Council, which represents diverse interests, including landowners, members of the scientific community and staff from state agencies. The advisory council recommends sites for acquisition, dedication and registration in the Washington Natural Area Preserve System. According to statute, lands eligible for inclusion under this system must be "valuable for the purposes of scientific research, teaching, as habitats of rare and vanishing species, as places of natural historic and natural interest and scenic beauty, and as living museums of the original heritage of the state."

In addition to the Department of Natural Resources, other state and federal agencies play an important role in protecting natural areas for ecological, scientific and educational purposes. Among these agencies, different designations are used for the lands that have been protected, including National Wildlife Refuges, Research Natural Areas, Natural Forests, Areas of Critical Environmental Concern, Special Interest Areas and Marine Biological Preserves.

To the casual observer, the distinctions between these designations and public agencies may blur. Yet despite the different names, all share a common purpose: to protect rare plant and animal species and representative ecosystems—the state's irreplaceable lifeboats of biodiversity—for generations to come.

*The beautiful small-flowered trillium is a state-sensitive forest plant protected by the Conservancy in Washington.*
(Mark Sheehan)

# T H E
# P R E S E R V E S

*"Like winds and sunsets,
wild things were taken
for granted until
progress began to do
away with them."*

—Aldo Leopold

# WHAT MAKES A CONSERVANCY PRESERVE?

*by Fayette Krause, Washington Land Steward*

Identification, acquisition and management.

This three-step approach provides the foundation for The Nature Conservancy's efforts to protect threatened and endangered species and ecosystems in the United States. Of course, it's all easier said than done. With so much land out there, where do you start?

The Conservancy has developed a program to address this question and to make the most efficient use of its limited land acquisition dollars. In every state, we have established statewide Natural Heritage Programs, generally in cooperation with an appropriate state agency. These programs attempt, in a scientific way, to determine which species or systems are at greatest risk and which occurrences of these rare "elements" are the highest quality and most suitable for protection.

Working through the Natural Heritage Program, scientists seek information about species and natural areas most in need of protection. Heritage Program staff gather data from members of the academic community, conservation groups and state and federal agencies. They collect scientific reports, historic narratives or other documents pertaining to these species and areas. They conduct extensive field

The uncommon pileated woodpecker carves its distinctive oval-shaped nest in the trunks of deciduous trees, deep within Washington's old-growth forests.
(Art Wolfe)

The black oystercatcher lays eggs in a nest that it scrapes out of rock chips and seashell fragments on Washington's more remote beaches.
(Keith Lazelle)

· 11 ·

research to verify where rare biological "elements" still exist and to evaluate their protection status statewide.

After analyzing and updating the information, Heritage Program staff draw up a prioritized list of natural areas most in need of protection. From this list, the Conservancy identifies its top candidates for acquisition and protection.

With priorities established, the Conservancy contacts landowners to determine whether they are willing to sell or donate property for a preserve. In some cases, acquisition can be a bit more complex. For instance, some owners of ecologically important land prefer to receive replacement land rather than cash for their property. We can help arrange an appropriate land exchange.

## STEWARDSHIP: MANAGING FOR THE FUTURE

Stewardship follows acquisition and usually takes one of two approaches: passive or active management. Under the former approach, the life of the preserve is allowed to evolve without human intervention. If this is the management objective, to protect the preserve and to monitor conditions within its boundaries may be all that is required.

But there are cases where preserving a special plant community or a particular species requires a more active role. For example, on our Yellow Island Preserve we have used controlled burning to perpetuate a rare native grassland community. Without fire or manual removal of woody plants, Yellow Island's open meadow would soon become forest or shrub habitat. Some native grasslands in Washington were maintained through natural wildfire and it is this influence we are attempting to mimic.

The Conservancy works with universities, providing research and educational opportunities where appropriate. Data gathered from our preserves can be used to answer questions about natural processes, allowing the Conservancy and others to better manage special lands and species.

*Controlled burning is an important management tool for keeping grasslands and other native plant communities in a natural state.*
(Stephen J. Krasemann)

We also cooperate with government agencies to achieve mutual objectives. The Skagit River Bald Eagle Natural Area is an excellent example of such cooperation. Here, the Conservancy and a number of federal and state agencies work closely with each other to guarantee that our combined efforts on the Skagit River provide the maximum benefit for wintering bald eagles.

When coordination with government agencies is required, or when research proposals must be evaluated, the Conservancy's staff perform these tasks. However, the stewardship of our preserves relies on a mix of staff and dedicated volunteers, a number of whom are preserve neighbors.

Volunteers provide a broad range of important services—from surveillance and weed eradication to public information and education. While volunteers come to the Conservancy from all walks of life, they all share one common interest: preserving our state's natural heritage. The contributions made by these dedicated individuals are absolutely essential to accomplishing the Conservancy's goals.

As stewards, we must also continually reevaluate our preserve boundaries. Do the current boundaries ensure the long-term preservation of the system or species we set out to protect? As we learn more about a species or better understand how a given system functions, we may determine that additional land is necessary to adequately protect them. At the Skagit River Bald Eagle Natural Area, for example, we've come to understand the importance of locating the eagles' communal night roosts (their "bedrooms") and identifying the critical salmon spawning areas (their "kitchens") within the eagles' primary wintering habitat. With this understanding, we've undertaken additional protective work.

During 1990-92 alone, government agencies and the Conservancy have dedicated an additional 3,500 acres on the Skagit for bald eagle protection. Added to the 1,065 acres already owned and managed by the Conservancy and the state Department of Wildlife, these recent dedications make the Skagit River Bald Eagle Natural Area the largest bald eagle reserve in the contiguous 48 states.

The Conservancy's first responsibility is to the land. Whenever we acquire a preserve, we make initial management decisions on whether human visitation is likely to have an adverse effect on the plants and animals living there. During their breeding seasons, certain animals (for example, some bald eagle pairs) are easily disturbed and need a high degree of isolation from people.

Some habitats and rare plants, especially those attractive to poachers, also need protection. Bunchgrass communities, for instance, are fragile and easily damaged by excessive foot traffic. Without measures to protect the bunchgrass communities on our preserves, we could easily degrade these grassland types.

In general, we manage the land conservatively to protect outstanding ecological values and the investments of our members.

We keep facilities and trails to a minimum; old structures and paths are often removed or closed off. The trails we do create are designed to direct visitors away from fragile areas to hardier sections of our preserves.

The following selection of 13 preserves are areas people may visit, subject to posted regulations. They represent a range of locations and habitat types and provide a sample of the Washington Chapter's holdings. They also include profiles of three areas established with Conservancy assistance that are protected by public agencies for ecological values.

We hope that when you visit preserves open to the public, you will gain a greater sense of our conservation mission. In addition to contributing financially, you may wish to become an active volunteer, working on a preserve or in the Washington Chapter's office. We appreciate your involvement, regardless of the form it takes.

Remember, only with your help can we maintain Washington's priceless system of natural areas for the generations to follow, and, equally important, the thousands of species that rely on our stewardship for their well-being.

We owe our children and other life forms nothing less than our very best efforts.

*The Columbian sharp-tailed grouse performs its elaborate courtship dance in the shrub-steppe grasslands of Eastern Washington. The Conservancy is working to preserve habitat for this once ubiquitous, but now rare bird.*
(Rich Landers)

Human visitors must
remember that
Conservancy
preserves are other
creatures' homes.
(Keith Lazelle)

# HANDLE WITH CARE

## RESPECTING THE PRESERVES

The Nature Conservancy's preserves are private properties, managed to protect native species and ecosystems. Whenever a property is acquired through the support of members and friends, the Conservancy makes the commitment to protect and safeguard the fragile characteristics of the preserve.

It would not be responsible to allow activities that could erode the very features the Conservancy has set out to protect. Consequently, some preserves must be closed to visitation. Others are open only during certain seasons or have special restrictions.

Information about seasonal closures and other special use regulations at individual preserves follow. Up-to-date information on all preserves can be obtained from the Washington Chapter office.

While on our preserves, visitors must respect the land and its wildlife at all times. They must also respect the rights of owners of adjacent private property. Only low-impact activities—walking, bird watching, nature study and photography—are permitted on Washington's Conservancy lands. Prior written approval must be obtained from the Conservancy before any group field trips, educational programs or research activities are conducted on a preserve.

Visitors are also asked to show their respect for the preserves by limiting the size of their groups, parking in designated areas and walking only on established trails. When encountering wildlife, special care must be taken: under no circumstances should animals be pursued, nor should visitors approach too close and harass the animals.

## PRESERVE RESTRICTIONS

The following restrictions are in effect on Conservancy preserves in Washington:

- No hunting, fishing or trapping
- No collecting plants or animals or their remains
- No camping
- No campfires
- No smoking
- No horses
- No bicycles or other off-road vehicles
- No pets (with the exception of seeing-eye dogs)
- Preserves are open dawn to dusk only.

When visiting, come prepared. The preserves have no restrooms or drinking water. Wear comfortable footwear suitable for hiking—no heavy, cleated boots, please. Pack rain gear, sunscreen and insect repellent for protection. For a longer hike, outfit yourself with a map, compass, first aid kit and a full water bottle. Of course, remember to bring your camera, binoculars and this book or other regional nature guides. Above all, take your time and enjoy nature's gifts!

*By showing respect for the land and its wildlife, bird watchers and other preserve visitors can help the Conservancy with its preservation goals.*
*(Gordon Todd)*

# BOOTS SATTERLEE

# BLACK RIVER PRESERVE

*With its dark, inky appearance, the Black River lives up to its name.*
*(Keith Lazelle)*

With a lowland lake as its main source, the Black River shows a dramatically different face from other rivers in the state, most of which are fed by melting snow. Flowing gently into the Chehalis River southwest of Olympia, the Black meanders through a vast, largely impenetrable swamp. The land on either side of its banks represents one of the most extensive, untouched riparian environments in Western Washington.

Reachable only by kayak, canoe or other small boat, the preserve contains an environment unlike any other in the state. Rising up from the soggy ground are mixed stands of red alder and distinctive Oregon ash, a handsome hardwood tree that grows to a height of 50 feet. Beneath these trees spreads a dense thicket of Pacific ninebark, red-osier dogwood and willow.

The thicket makes foot travel difficult, yet it creates a safe, near-impenetrable home for swamp dwellers such as the river otter, beaver and mink. Stilt-legged waders, the American bittern and green-backed heron, hunt silently in the calm water at the river's edge, while the yellow warbler and other native songbirds flit among the branches on the banks. For an easy paddle through land largely unaltered by humans, the Black River is ideal.

Immediately across the channel from the Conservancy's property on the Black River is the Black River Habitat Management Area, another vital Washington swampland. Managed by the Washington Department of Wildlife, this protected area comprises more than 300 acres.

The history of the Conservancy's preserve is a personal one. In 1957, Boots Satterlee traded four city lots in Seattle's North Beach neighborhood for 77 acres of shrub swamp on the Black River. Later, she lived on this out-of-the-way acreage—first in an A-frame cabin without electricity or running water, later in a more sophisticated cabin with amenities—for nearly 20 years.

Boots loved her land dearly. After she died in 1986, her children donated 21.5 acres of her land to The Nature Conservancy. Their generous donation ensured that a portion of the land would be preserved in its natural state, creating a fitting, permanent memorial to their adventuresome mother.

The qualities of life that lured her from the city to the country continue to impress visitors to the Black River.

*Limbs of a familiar streamside dweller, the red-osier dogwood, are reflected in the Black River's placid waters.*
*(Keith Lazelle)*

*A near-impenetrable thicket lines both sides of the Black River's banks.*
(Keith Lazelle)

**Directions:** *From Olympia, drive 12 miles south on Interstate 5 to the Rochester exit (Highway 12). Follow Highway 12 west through the town of Rochester. Proceed approximately three miles past Albany Street to a boat launch on the left. This site and another near Highway 121 (approximately six miles upriver) are the only means of access to the site. Both boat launches are operated by the Washington Department of Wildlife for access to its management area.*

**Visitor access:** *Open year-round. Access is by private boat only. Preserve is dense shrub swamp with no trails, best viewed from water. All other preserve restrictions apply (see page 16).*

River otter

Boat Launch

Littlerock Road SW

Black River

Moon Road SW

Black River Preserve

State Route 121

Boat Launch

N

Albany Street SW

US Highway 12

to Interstate 5 →

Cattails border
wetland shrub thicket
and Sitka spruce,
the dominant features
of the Robert W. Little
Preserve.
(Keith Lazelle)

Keen hearing and a
camouflage coat are the major
assets of the endangered
Columbian white-tailed deer.
(Keith Lazelle)

# ROBERT W. LITTLE PRESERVE

# PUGET ISLAND

Bordered by the Westport Channel of the Columbia River and the adjoining mouth of Grove Slough, the Robert W. Little Preserve on Puget Island provides native tidal spruce swampland important for the survival of the endangered Columbian white-tailed deer. A densely wooded shrub swamp, the preserve is also home to towering shaggy Sitka spruce trees.

In addition to sheltering the deer, the Little Preserve serves as a sanctuary for beaver, raccoon, great blue heron and other wetland wildlife. Seasonally, it also becomes home to numerous migratory bird species.

Not long ago, all of Puget Island was covered with trees. Now most of this land on the Columbia River has been logged, diked and converted to pasture and croplands. Today, native woodlands account for less than 300 of the island's 8,000 acres.

Accompanying the demise of riverine woodland habitat along the Columbia River has been the decline of the Columbian white-tailed deer. Historically, the Columbian, one of 38 subspecies of white-tailed deer in the Americas, ranged from the southern end of Puget Sound to the Willamette Valley of Oregon. Today, only two populations can be found, one near Roseburg, Oregon, and another on a few small islands and in isolated areas of the lower Columbia River near Cathlamet, Washington.

Efforts to save the Columbian white-tailed deer from extinction began in 1972, when the U.S. Fish and Wildlife Service (USFWS) established the 4,800-acre Julia Butler Hansen Refuge for the Columbian White-Tailed Deer near Cathlamet. By securing habitat for a minimum of 400 deer in at least three viable herds, USFWS hopes to one day achieve the recovery goal for this federally endangered animal.

The Nature Conservancy has cooperated with USFWS to support the habitat protection for the Columbian white-tailed deer. To expand protected deer habitat, the Washington Chapter of the Conservancy acquired this natural wooded area on Puget Island—a 30-acre peninsula of undiked river flood plain. In 1991, the family of Robert W. Little donated funds to buy this property to commemorate Mr. Little and his strong belief that the Earth and its natural diversity should be preserved.

Total numbers of the deer in the lower Columbia River population have increased in recent years. However, the deer have shown no ability to expand their range and establish new, viable subpopulations outside of their current lower Columbia River habitat—a range to which they have been limited for many decades. Until long-term trends for comeback of the deer can be established, the Little Preserve will remain a valuable haven for the endangered white-tailed deer.

*Red-osier dogwood*

Robert W. Little Preserve

Crossdike Road

Grove Slough

Birnie Slough Road

Columbia River

Welcome Slough

South Welcome Slough Road

N

**Directions:** From Cathlamet, take State Highway 409 south approximately 1.5 miles to West Birnie Slough Road on Puget Island. Turn west and proceed for approximately three-quarters of a mile to Crossdike Road junction. Follow Crossdike Road approximately 1.5 miles to the junction with North Welcome Slough Road. The preserve lies along North Welcome Slough Road at this point for one-fifth of a mile.

**Visitor access:** Open February to August only. Park on North Welcome Slough Road. Preserve is densely wooded shrub swamp with no trails, most easily viewed from road. All other preserve restrictions apply (see page 16).

A languid low-flier, this northern harrier (or marsh hawk) surveys its surroundings from a Puget Island perch. By day, this migratory bird of prey searches nearby fields for rodents and small birds. It roosts on the ground at night.

(Keith Lazelle)

# CHUCKANUT ISLAND

# CYRUS GATES MEMORIAL PRESERVE

Despite its proximity to the mainland of Whatcom County, Chuckanut Island supports vegetation more closely resembling that of the San Juan Islands. Douglas-fir (some well over 250 years old), grand fir, madrone and western redcedar form the forest canopy of this flat-topped, five-acre island. The understory is dominated by salal, ocean spray and snowberry.

Sculpted sandstone walls rise above an intertidal area rich in marine life that rings the island. Barnacles, snails, rock crabs, scallops, sea cucumbers, limpets, hermit crabs, butter clams, cockles, horse clams and blue mud shrimp are just a few of the 55 marine inverte-brate species found here. As scientists continue to study the island's intertidal habitats, the list of marine invertebrates continues to grow.

Surfbirds, which winter in flocks of two dozen or more in Chuckanut Bay, frequently perch on the island's rocky shore. In flight, they share the sky with two bald eagles that nest on the island.

Because there is no source of fresh water on the island, human impact has been slight. A small opening in the forest is all that remains to remind visitors that people once attempted to eke out a living on this out-of-the-way isle.

Frances Gates McCord and Cyrus Kingsley Gates donated this haven in Chuckanut Bay to the Washington Chapter of the Conservancy in 1976, naming it after their father, Cyrus Gates. Today, the residents of nearby Chuckanut Drive are strongly protective of the Cyrus Gates Memorial Preserve and the mainland shores, as well. The island's volunteer steward frequently travels by motorboat to care for the island, keeping a constant watch for campfires and campers, neither of which is allowed.

*Volunteer preserve stewards like George Garlick of Chuckanut Island have proven themselves invaluable in protecting Conservancy lands.*
(Charles Nishida)

*Deposited over time by tidal currents, a small spit of fine gravel and crushed shell projects from Chuckanut Island's sculpted sandstone walls.*
(Keith Lazelle)

*Western starflower blossoms appear
each April on Chuckanut Island.*
(Keith Lazelle)

**Left**: *Among the most
handsome of coastal
waterfowl, the harlequin
duck dives for small crabs,
shrimp, shellfish and an
occasional fish.*
(Art Wolfe)

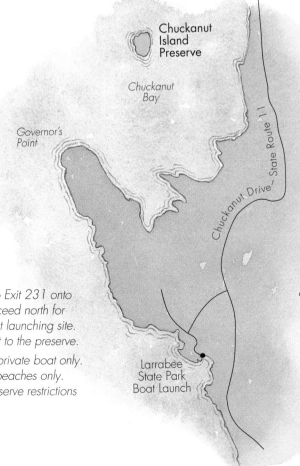

**Directions:** *From Bellingham, take Interstate 5 to Exit 231 onto
Route 11 (also known as Chuckanut Drive). Proceed north for
14.4 miles to Larrabee State Park, a public boat launching site.
Continue north by boat around Governor's Point to the preserve.*

**Visitor access:** *Open year-round. Access is by private boat only.
Boats may be beached on northeast and west beaches only.
Stay on foot trail that circles island. All other preserve restrictions
apply (see page 16).*

# DISHMAN HILLS

## PRESERVE

*Wispy blooms of prairie smoke avens catch the hillside's faint breezes.*
(Keith Lazelle)

In spring, the slopes explode with blossoms. Blue violets peer from shady nooks, while magenta shooting stars and purple larkspurs accent the grasslands. As summer approaches, blue camas, yellow glacier lilies and bluebells appear. Long after the other wildflowers—buttercups, grass widows, trillium and yellowbells—have faded, the slopes of the Conservancy's Dishman Hills Preserve continue to glow with the gold of native bunchgrasses.

Faced with such botanical splendor, it's hard to imagine that the Dishman Hills are but a few minutes' drive from downtown Spokane or that the adjacent Ina H. Johnston Natural Area is bounded on three sides by residential and commercial development.

The Dishman Hills Preserve rests on some of the oldest geological formations in the state. Its granite hills were sculpted by the great Missoula flood that followed the last ice age, about 15,000 years ago. As water raced across what is now the southeastern portion of the state, it swept the soil off the land, carving a series of channels and creating the scablands by exposing the hard rock beneath.

Gradually, over thousands of years, animals and plants returned to the present-day Dishman Hills, repopulating two distinctive zones

*Right: The bark of mature ponderosa pine is rich orange, textured with large, plate-like scales. The bark of immature trees is considerably darker with less defined plates.*
(Bonnie Lee Sharpe)

One of 52 butterfly species recorded at Dishman Hills, this common blue touches down on a balsamroot leaf.
(Keith Lazelle)

*Directions:* From downtown Spokane, take Interstate 90 east to the Argonne Road exit and proceed south to Sprague Avenue. Turn right and drive one-quarter of a mile to Sargent Road. Turn left and continue straight on Sargent Road to its terminus in the Camp Caro parking lot.

*Visitor access:* Open year-round. Take foot trail from Camp Caro parking lot. Please remain on trails. All other preserve restrictions apply (see page 16).

of life. The hills' lower slopes are now clothed in stands of ponderosa pine, Douglas-fir and grassland plants, while a narrow forest of western larch, grand fir and western hemlock now straddles the small creek on the east side of Tower Mountain. Rare, threatened and endangered animals and plants—including the rubber boa, Compton's tortoiseshell butterfly and *Howellia*, a member of the harebell plant family—are among the inhabitants of these two zones.

In 1967, the Washington Chapter of The Nature Conservancy worked with the Dishman Hills Association, a small group of Spokane citizens, to buy 80 acres of land. Two years later, Ina H. Johnston, a prominent Spokane philanthropist, donated $30,000 to the county. With matching funds from state and federal sources, an additional 124 acres of valuable Dishman Hills habitat was acquired.

Today, the Dishman Hills Natural Resource Conservation Area is spread over 530 acres, with parcels owned by the state Department of Natural Resources, the Dishman Hills Association, Spokane County Parks and Recreation and the Washington Chapter of The Nature Conservancy. The lodge at Camp Caro on the county's portion of the site serves as a nature center and several trails lead visitors through brightly colored fields of wild blooms.

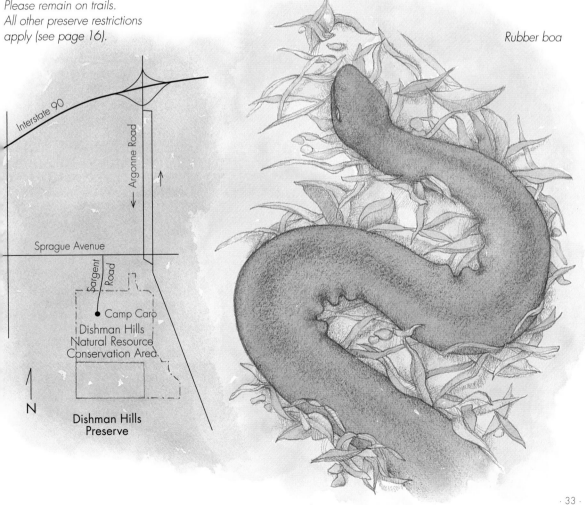

Rubber boa

Interstate 90

Argonne Road

Sprague Avenue

Sargent Road

Camp Caro

Dishman Hills Natural Resource Conservation Area

N

Dishman Hills Preserve

# WALDRON ISLAND

## PRESERVE

In 1972, the residents of Waldron Island contributed $28,000 to help preserve the character of 250 acres on Cowlitz Bay. A piece of their island was going to be sold for development. With the sale of land, the residents feared, would come electricity, telephones and ferry service—elements that the oldest citizens of the island had blissfully forgone for decades.

Hoping to stem the tide of development, the residents approached the Washington Chapter of The Nature Conservancy. They pooled their funds with those of the Conservancy to purchase the parcel of land on Cowlitz Bay from its syndicate of owners. The land acquired was a complete world of island ecology that ranged from beachfront to marshland to forest.

Especially valuable from an ecological standpoint are the Waldron Island Preserve's 4,000 feet of pristine beach and its 52 acres of freshwater marsh. The latter acreage constitutes one of the finest, most diverse freshwater marsh systems in San Juan County. Three separate areas of cattail, mare's tail and marsh grasses create a green oasis for a wealth of migratory water birds. Cinnamon, blue-winged and green-winged teal are particularly fond of the habitats created by these tall wetland plants. So are coots, rails, great blue heron and an occasional whistling swan. A thicket of rose bushes interspersed with Douglas spirea provides a safe haven for muskrats and river otters, which build dens at the marsh's edge.

Strewn with bleached driftwood and logs, the sandy beach of the Waldron Island Preserve is one of the longest in the San Juans. Like the preserve's marshes, it is popular with winged visitors. Sandpipers, dunlin, plovers and other shorebirds pick their way along the beach at low tide. The seafood smorgasbord of cockles, sandworms and crabs attracts several species of gulls. The flute-like laughter of common and Arctic loons is carried to shore by the strong sea winds.

Bald eagles can be seen soaring high over the beach. Other raptors—Cooper's and sharp-shinned hawks—circle in the preserve's nearby meadow. On a clear day, both hawks and humans enjoy one of the most spectacular views in the San Juan Islands, with unbroken vistas of the snow-capped peaks of the Olympic Mountain Range to the south and majestic Mount Baker and the Cascade Mountain Range to the northeast.

*Directions: The preserve sits
on Cowlitz Bay, between
Sandy Point and Point Disney.*

*Visitor access: Open year-
round. Access is by private
boat only. Stay on beach and
short trail that heads east from
the beach. Tidelands are
included in the preserve and
are closed to the taking of
any life forms or materials.
All other preserve restrictions
apply (see page 16).*

*Pigeon guillemot*

# SKAGIT RIVER
## 🌿
## BALD EAGLE NATURAL AREA

As the stark, somber gray of November replaces October's brilliant yellow and red, bald eagles begin returning to their favored wintering grounds along the Skagit River. Gradually the population builds to several hundred, peaking in mid-January.

This impressive winter gathering of bald eagles, which is one of the four largest in the contiguous 48 states, coincides with the spawning runs of chum salmon on the Skagit River. The carcasses of the spent fish, washed onto gravel bars and in shallow water, are a major food source for the eagles.

As the supply of carrion diminishes in this eagle "kitchen," bald eagle numbers dwindle, until by mid-March all of the birds have dispersed.

The bald eagle is listed as a threatened species in Washington state and an endangered species in 43 other states. Protection of this rare bird has been one of the chief concerns of the Washington Chapter of The Nature Conservancy over the last decade. Today, the Conservancy, the state Department of Wildlife and several other agencies own more than 4,500 acres of prime bald eagle wintering habitat along the Skagit River.

Efforts of the Conservancy to set aside habitat for wintering eagles began in 1976, with the initial acquisition of 875 acres near Rockport in the North Cascades. In 1983, an additional 38 acres was obtained. This new acreage included privately held property between Illabot Creek and Illabot Slough, considered the most significant chum salmon spawning segments of the Skagit River. The land now serves as an important eagle retreat.

In 1990, the purchase of 151 acres of land surrounding Barnaby Slough increased the Conservancy's holdings within the Skagit River Bald Eagle Natural Area to 464 acres. Barnaby Slough is one of the most heavily frequented bald eagle communal night roosting areas, or eagle "bedrooms," along the Skagit. Census figures from 1988 and 1989 show that scores of birds seek shelter in the slough's thick stands of mature cottonwood, alder and bigleaf maple. The site also serves as

*After a morning meal of salmon, bald eagles return to their secure, riverside perches to preen.*
*(Art Wolfe)*

an off-river perch area during the day. Because the roost is located near the eagles' feeding areas, the birds do not have to travel far or expend much energy to reach their food source.

The Washington Chapter of the Conservancy continues to actively protect the bald eagle. Staff participate on the Skagit Bald Eagle Advisory Committee, which includes representatives from Seattle City Light, U.S. Bureau of Land Management, U.S. Forest Service and state departments of Wildlife, Fisheries, Natural Resources and Public Instruction. During the eagle wintering period, a preserve steward conducts a weekly bird census, gives guided tours of the area and makes presentations to school and community groups.

*Directions: From Seattle, take Interstate 5 north to Exit 230. Follow Highway 20 through Burlington and continue 36 miles to Rockport. Eagle viewing sites are the Washington Eddy lookout, 1 mile east of Rockport on Highway 20, and a highway pullout, 1.3 miles farther east.*

*Visitor access: Public viewing of eagles is confined to the Washington Eddy lookout and Highway 20 pullout listed above, plus the Skagit View Trail at Rockport State Park. Speak quietly and minimize movement to avoid disturbing eagles. Visitors floating the river must launch from Marblemount between 10 a.m. and noon only. Do not beach between Rocky Creek and Rockport; this includes gravel bars. Float quietly and minimize movement. All other preserve restrictions apply (see page 16).*

*A stand of red alder lines the Skagit River, providing shade and helping to lower water temperatures for salmon during hot summer months.*
(Keith Lazelle)

*A solitary bald eagle scans the horizon from a secure perch along the Skagit River*
(Keith Lazelle)

Chum salmon

# FOULWEATHER
# B L U F F
🌿
# P R E S E R V E

Two miles northwest of Hansville, near the tip of the Kitsap Peninsula, a stand of 70-foot-tall red alders welcomes visitors to the Foulweather Bluff Preserve. Just beyond this stand is another grove, where second-growth Douglas-fir and western redcedar predominate.

Once common in the wet bottomlands of Western Washington, old-growth forests containing redcedar have declined significantly during the 20th century. Protected from future logging by the Washington Chapter of The Nature Conservancy, the cedars near Hansville will eventually dominate the preserve's forest.

The lowland forest, with its lush native understory of ocean spray, salmonberry, sword fern and salal, supports many different bird species. Winter wrens inhabit the forest floor, red-breasted nuthatches work the tree trunks, and chestnut-backed chickadees forage for insects on the conifer bows. The ringing call of the pileated woodpecker resounds through the trees.

The forest, however, is just one of several distinct habitats at Foulweather Bluff. The preserve's single most important feature is its brackish marsh, where great blue heron silently stalk their prey and bald eagles and osprey soar effortlessly overhead. Within the marsh is a mosaic of wetland plants, with common spike-rush and seacoast bulrush at one end and hardstem bulrush and cattail at the other.

The marsh and its surrounding watershed are separated from the salt water of Hood Canal by a raised barrier of sand. Beyond this

*Above*: Flowers of Pacific silverweed, a native cinquefoil, complete this Zen-like arrangement of driftwood and stones.

*Left*: This madrone is living testimony that Nature can overcome nearly every obstacle—even the force of gravity.
(Keith Lazelle)

*Flocks of lesser scaup gather at Foulweather Bluff, an important stopover on their migrations to and from breeding grounds in the far north. Only experienced birders can distinguish this fowl from its fellow traveler, the greater scaup.*
(Keith Lazelle)

natural berm, a 3,700-foot-long beach draws hikers and nature enthusiasts, and extensive tideflats offer opportunities for close examination of intertidal life. Near shore, white and black bufflehead ducks court every spring. In winter, loons, grebes, scoters and other seabirds raft at the surface of Hood Canal's cold sea.

The combination of forest, marsh, beach and sea makes the Foulweather Bluff Preserve one of the most valuable wildlife havens on the Kitsap Peninsula. In the early 1930s, after most old-growth forests on the peninsula had been logged, Dr. Erroll Rawson and his brother Ralph purchased 86 acres between Hood Canal and Twin Spits Road. The upland area, which surrounds the biologically productive marsh, regenerated naturally and by the mid-1960s, a mixed second-growth forest was well established.

The Rawsons' desire to protect the area's wildlife led them to donate the property south of Twin Spits Road to The Nature Conservancy, establishing the Foulweather Bluff Preserve in 1967. The brothers then worked with the Washington Chapter to acquire adjacent parcels of land from four other public-spirited families in the area. They later established a trust fund for the long-term management of the preserve.

Today the preserve contains 93 acres of marsh, beach and woodland. It stands as a testimonial to a committed group of landowners who ensured wildlife a continuing home at Foulweather Bluff.

*Foulweather Bluff's single most important feature is its brackish marsh, a sheltering, moist haven for insects, fish, birds and mammals.*
*(Harold E. Malde)*

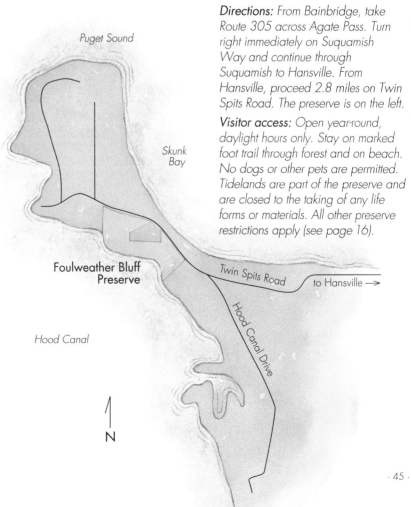

*Directions: From Bainbridge, take Route 305 across Agate Pass. Turn right immediately on Suquamish Way and continue through Suquamish to Hansville. From Hansville, proceed 2.8 miles on Twin Spits Road. The preserve is on the left.*

*Visitor access: Open year-round, daylight hours only. Stay on marked foot trail through forest and on beach. No dogs or other pets are permitted. Tidelands are part of the preserve and are closed to the taking of any life forms or materials. All other preserve restrictions apply (see page 16).*

Puget Sound

Skunk Bay

Foulweather Bluff Preserve

Twin Spits Road

to Hansville →

Hood Canal

Hood Canal Drive

N

# PIERCE ISLAND
## PRESERVE

The saloon that old-timers claim once stood on the island's high ground has vanished, allegedly washed away by the great flood of 1894. Also gone are the fishwheels, the water-driven devices whose rotating baskets scooped salmon from the majestic Columbia River. What remain are the shady woodlands of black cottonwood, willow and ash and the insects that gave The Nature Conservancy's 85-acre Pierce Island Preserve its original name—Mosquito Island.

Pierce Island is underlain by cobble and coarse gravel, reportedly deposited after impounded river waters broke through the Table Mountain landslide deposit of basalt rock that had temporarily dammed the Columbia 1,200 years ago. Overlying this cobble and gravel are more recent deposits of finer gravels, sands and silts.

Because humans played a relatively small part in the island's long history, Pierce is considered among the best remaining natural islands in the Columbia River Gorge. It is one of the few in the region that have not been destroyed or significantly altered by conversion to other uses. However, in the early 1980s, even this island was threatened by a proposal to clearcut its forest to create a disposal site for dredge spoils from the construction of Bonneville Dam.

From its willow perch, the yellow warbler fills the air of Pierce Island with song.

(Keith Lazelle)

*Osprey*

Transforming Pierce Island into a dredge disposal site would have meant the loss of an important river floodplain, including nesting and overwintering habitat for the Great Basin subspecies of Canada goose. Other animal inhabitants, including great blue heron, osprey and beaver would also have suffered from the destruction of the island's habitats.

In addition, a population of a rare plant species would have been jeopardized. Persistentsepal yellowcress (a member of the mustard family) grows on the island's cobble-gravel shoreline. Fewer than a dozen locations are known for this species in all of North America, and only one—Pierce Island—offers the plant any formal protection.

In 1984, the Conservancy bought the island at a bargain price from the Knappton Corporation, a marine transportation company headquartered in Portland, Oregon. The preserve and its adjoining shorelands, which comprise as much as 200 acres when the water level of the Columbia is low, now lie within the federal Columbia Gorge Scenic Area. Situated in one of the last major free-flowing stretches of the Columbia River, Pierce Island offers spectacular views of the Columbia Gorge and Beacon Rock.

*The endangered persistent-sepal yellowcress is found on only two stretches of the Columbia River in Washington, including the Conservancy's Pierce Island Preserve.*
*(Russ Jolley)*

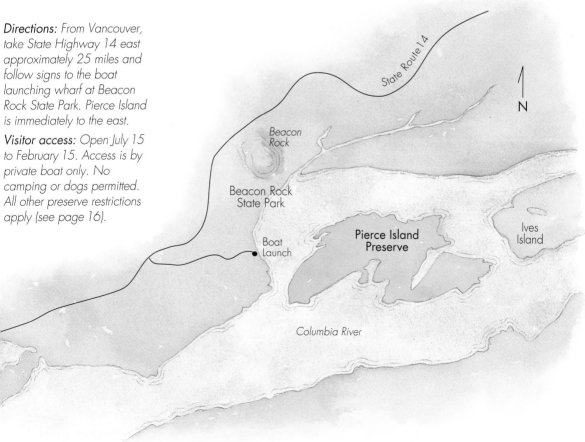

**Directions:** From Vancouver, take State Highway 14 east approximately 25 miles and follow signs to the boat launching wharf at Beacon Rock State Park. Pierce Island is immediately to the east.

**Visitor access:** Open July 15 to February 15. Access is by private boat only. No camping or dogs permitted. All other preserve restrictions apply (see page 16).

State Route 14

N

Beacon Rock

Beacon Rock State Park

Boat Launch

Pierce Island Preserve

Ives Island

Columbia River

# R O S E  C R E E K

*❧*

# P R E S E R V E

Above Rose Creek, rolling Palouse wheat fields shimmer golden in the August sun. By fall, only stubble remains, but in the bottomland that forms The Nature Conservancy's Rose Creek Preserve, an array of autumnal colors brings the landscape to life. Yellow-leafed aspen contrast sharply with the reddish-brown foliage of the black hawthorn, while nearby, skeletal stalks of cow parsnip await the leveling blasts of winter wind.

The Rose Creek Preserve is one of the best remaining examples of this rare plant community, which, even prior to grazing and farming, covered less than five percent of Whitman County. On the preserve, black hawthorn grows to a height of 15 feet or more. The understory of cow parsnip grows to a height of six feet, creating a cool sanctuary for wildlife during hot summer months.

George and Bess Hudson, founders of The Nature Conservancy's former Inland Empire Chapter, donated the first preserve to the Conservancy in 1966. When purchased by the Hudsons in 1957, the 22 acres of land had been overgrazed. The couple allowed the land to recover, and today the preserve is recognized as containing one of the best black hawthorn/cow parsnip riparian areas left in the entire Palouse.

*A patchwork quilt of farmland is draped across Smoot Hill, one of the more prominent features of the landscape near Rose Creek.*
*(Keith Lazelle)*

At Rose Creek and a few other sites, the relationship between the black hawthorn and quaking aspen is particularly complex. As the aspen grows, it shades out the hawthorn, which dies back to rootstocks, only to re-emerge when the short-lived aspen falls victim to heart rot. Following a dormant period, the aspen sprouts again and the cycle repeats.

Part of the Palouse River drainage, the Rose Creek Preserve is surrounded by a sea of wheat. Rose Creek bisects the preserve, offering life-sustaining water to more than 100 species of birds. In winter, long-eared owls roost in the dense hawthorn thickets as red-tailed hawks hunt the adjoining hills. Some of the less common Eastern Washington birds, such as catbirds and black-chinned hummingbirds, are also attracted to Rose Creek.

*Despite the built-in protection
their quills afford, porcupines
are shy and retiring animals.*
*(Keith Lazelle)*

The preserve supports more than 250 species of vascular plants and provides food and habitat to mammals ranging in size from the diminutive shrew and vole to the much larger porcupine, coyote and white-tailed deer. All of these animals are suffering from habitat loss and degradation in the Palouse.

Black hawthorn

*Directions:* From Pullman, head north on Route 27 an turn left on the Albion-Pullman Road. In Albion, turn right on Main Street, which becomes Old Albion Road (gravel), and proceed 2.8 miles. Turn left on Four Mile Road and continue, bearing left, for a half mile to the preserve, which is on the right.

*Visitor access:* Open year-round. Stay on marked trail that leads from small parking area. No dogs or other pets permitted. All other preserve restrictions apply (see page 16).

Four Mile Creek

Rose Creek
Preserve

Four Mile Road

N

Smoot Hill

Old Albion Road

Rose Creek

to Albion

# YELLOW ISLAND

# PRESERVE

From late March to early June, wildflowers carpet Yellow Island. Colors emerge and recede, beginning with yellow buttercups and delicate white fawn lilies. Cryptic brown and green chocolate lilies, purple shooting stars and blue camas contribute their colors to the already brilliant palette of nature's hues.

Long known to passengers aboard Washington's San Juan Islands ferries for its dramatic display of spring wildflowers, 10-acre Yellow Island is among the most colorful of The Nature Conservancy's holdings. The small preserve's springtime display of floral profusion and diversity is greater than that of any other similar-sized area in the 170-island San Juan archipelago.

More than 150 species of wildflowers, including broadleafed shooting star, hairy Indian paintbrush and brittle cactus (the only cactus species native to Western Washington), can be found here. Many of these plants occur throughout the San Juans, but only Yellow Island, with its open fescue meadows and the absence of resident grazing animals, hosts such dense populations.

Yellow Island is long and thin, with sand spits at each end, a belt of evergreens across the middle and grassy meadows that overlook the two spits. Contained on this tiny piece of land are representatives

Jones Island

Orcas

Island

Deer
Harbor

Orcas
Island

McConnell
Island

Crane Island

Orcas
Ferry Landing

Yellow
Island
Preserve

Shaw
Island

N

San Juan
Island

Friday Harbor
Ferry Landing

of nearly all of the important floral and faunal groups of the San Juans. Bald eagles frequently perch in the island's tallest trees, and harbor seals haul out on the island's twin spits between tides. Highly patterned harlequin ducks forage near shore, taking advantage of the prolific life in the intertidal zone.

Farther from the island's wave-swept, weather-beaten coast, bold black and white killer whales travel in large family groups called pods. Other marine mammals—minke whales, harbor porpoise and Dall's porpoise—swim in the nutrient-laden currents that bathe Yellow Island.

When Lewis and Elizabeth ("Tib") Dodd bought the island in 1947, they were determined to live in peaceful coexistence with nature. An avid reader of Thoreau, Lewis Dodd strongly believed in self-sufficiency. After living in a tent for two years, he and Tib moved into a house, a small rustic cabin they built with beach-combed timber and rock. This distinctive landmark remains basically unaltered to this day. As the Dodds cultivated a small garden, planted a few fruit trees and grape vines and raised chickens and pigeons for meat, they left the island's wealth of animals and plants largely undisturbed. Their years on the island were testimony to a lifestyle in harmony with nature.

After her husband's death in 1960, Tib continued to live on the island during the summer months, spending winters at their daughter's home in Seattle. Her decision to sell the island to the Conservancy's Washington Chapter in 1980 was greeted enthusiastically by her family and San Juan Island neighbors. Today, a pair of bronze memorial plaques for the Dodds, their cabin (which now serves as a home for the stewards that manage most of the Conservancy's holdings in the San Juans) and a few inconspicuous nature trails serve to remind us of Yellow Island's former occupants.

*The black oystercatcher's chisel-shaped bill is well suited for prying limpets, chitons and other shellfish from rocks at low tide.*
*(Keith Lazelle)*

**Directions:** *Yellow Island is a 20-minute boat ride from San Juan Island's Friday Harbor.*

**Visitor access:** *Open year-round. Access is by private boat only on east and west spits and on south beach east of cabin. Stay on established trails. All other preserve restrictions apply (see page 16).*

# MIMA MOUNDS NATURAL AREA PRESERVE

*Mimicking natural fire, Northwest Native Americans burned their prairie, encouraging the growth of edible camas bulbs. Without fire, the forest now creeps ever closer to these lily-like blue flowers.*
(Keith Lazelle)

*Western meadowlark*

**Directions:** *From Olympia, drive south on Interstate 5 to exit 95. Follow State Route 121 west to Littlerock. Continue through town, then turn right at Waddell Creek Road. Preserve entrance is on the left.*

**Visitor access:** *Open year-round during daylight hours. Motorized vehicles, horses or pets are not allowed beyond the parking lot. A picnic area on the mounds accommodates small groups.*

Local farmers call them "baffling bumps." Officially they are Mima Mounds—six-foot-tall landforms that dot the landscape south of Olympia. The origin of these strange, evenly spaced mounds is indeed baffling, having eluded scholars for 150 years.

One of the first to tackle the mystery of the Mima Mounds was Captain Charles Wilkes, leader of the United States Exploring Expedition that charted the Northwest. In 1841, Wilkes organized a journey specifically to see the Mima Mounds and, he hoped, unearth relics from what he perceived to be Indian burial grounds. Instead, Wilkes walked away from his unsuccessful dig, having found only a "pavement of stones" at the bottom of the mounds.

Since the days of Captain Wilkes, more than 150 scientific papers have questioned the origin of the mounds. From this sizable pile of literature, three dominant theories have emerged: that the mounds were built by pocket gophers or other small mammals that dug in the earth thousands of years ago; that the strong period of freezing and thawing that followed the departure of the glaciers (some 10,000 to 15,000 years ago) caused the earth to crack and bulge, slowly forming the mounds; or that the mounds were created by a severe earthquake, which shaped the unconsolidated soils that rested on the area's hard layer of bedrock into the many small mounds we see today.

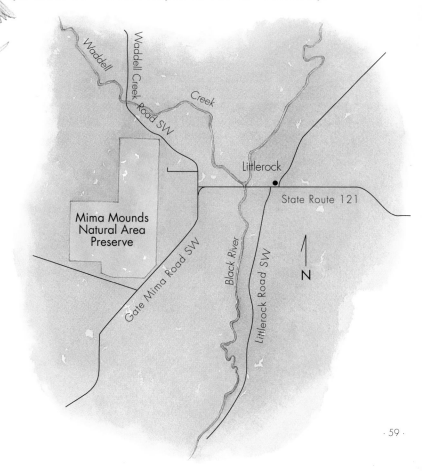

Punctured by camas
flowers, a thick carpet of
mosses and lichens spreads
over the Mima Mounds.
(Keith Lazelle)

Their puzzling origins aside, the 445-acre Mima Mounds Natural Area Preserve provides a fine example of an evolving prairie system. In pre-settlement times, the mounds were covered with prairie vegetation—grasses, mosses, lichens and herbs. But in the absence of wildfires and burning by Native Americans, the surrounding coniferous forest has slowly encroached on the grasslands, especially in the central and northern portions of the preserve.

Since 1910, the forest has advanced into the prairie at an estimated one-fourth to three-eighths of a mile per year. Left unchecked, the clusters of Douglas-fir and clumps of Scot's broom (a non-native plant, introduced to Washington in the mid-1800s) will radically change the complexion of the Mima Mounds Natural Area Preserve. Active management may be required to restore and maintain the native prairie.

Like most lowland areas in Washington's Puget Trough region, the Mima Mounds have been greatly altered by human hands. Prior to 1972, the Mima Mounds property belonged to the state's school trust, and the prairie was leased for livestock grazing. In 1972, The Nature Conservancy assumed the grazing lease from the state's school trust and assigned stewardship to The Evergreen State College. Three years later, DNR terminated the lease and, using funds provided by the Interagency Committee for Outdoor Recreation, purchased the land including the mounds from the school trust. The use of these funds required that components of public recreation be included in the new Mima Mounds Natural Area Preserve. To make the preserve more accessible to visitors, DNR has added an interpretive kiosk, marked nature trails and a paved half-mile course for the handicapped.

*Right*: Perched on a camas
bloom, an anise swallowtail
flexes its geometrically
patterned wings.
(Keith Lazelle)

The Dungeness is a long sand spit that is still growing. The leeward arc of this massive work-in-progress is a haven for wildlife. Its windswept outer shore is a long-distance beachwalker's dream. (Keith Lazelle)

American wigeon, bufflehead, green-winged teal, surf scoter, horned grebe, Caspian tern. After a day at Dungeness National Wildlife Refuge, a bird watcher's checklist begins to sound like a complete inventory of Washington's winged, web-footed migrants.

As many as 30,000 waterfowl stop briefly at Dungeness each fall on their journey south for the winter and each spring as they return north. The majority stop for a few days to eat and rest before resuming their journeys. Others—as many as 10,000 of these long-distance travelers in any one year—may spend the entire winter, diving, dabbling and foraging for food in the productive habitats that line Dungeness Spit.

Formed from eroding soil and shaped by wind and water currents 10,000 to 20,000 years ago, Dungeness Spit stretches five and one-half miles along the Strait of Juan de Fuca near the town of Sequim. The spit's distal end is still growing at a rate of nearly fourteen and a half feet per year. Looping back to create a natural breakwater against the strong ocean waves and winds, the spit has created a safe haven for an abundance of plants and animals.

Submerged meadows of eelgrass serve as feeding and rearing grounds for salmon, clams, crabs and many other marine organisms. Where water and land meet is a sandy beach littered with driftwood, home to an assortment of shore birds. Here, during the spring migration, as many as 8,000 to 12,000 shore birds stop over. Seven gull species also visit the refuge, sharing their coastal turf with loon, great blue heron and grebes.

One of the most important visitors to Dungeness is the black brant, a diminutive species of goose that depends on aquatic plants, primarily eel grass and sea lettuce, for its food. As acre upon acre of coastal wetland is lost from the Pacific coast of North America, the brant population has plummeted. The population of 13,000 to 15,000 brant that now winter in Washington is far below the historic winter population, once as high as 30,000 birds. For the northward migrating brant, the nurturing waters of Dungeness Spit are much-

*Along with dunlin, western sandpipers are the most seasonally abundant birds on the Washington coast. During spring and fall migrations, they gather by the thousands on beaches adjacent to estuaries and tide flats, probing the soft sediments with their tweezer-like bills.*
*(Keith Lazelle)*

*Habitat losses have caused black brant populations to plummet.*

**Directions:** *From U.S. Highway 101 west of Sequim, drive north for three miles on Kitchen-Dick Lane, then turn right on Lotzgesell Road and left into the Dungeness Recreation Area. The road ends at the refuge parking lot. The nearest public boat ramp is located off the refuge on Cline Spit.*

**Visitor access:** *Open year-round during daylight hours; entrance fee is $2 per family. Boating, fishing and clamming are permitted, subject to state regulations. Motorized vehicles, bicycles, pets or fires are not permitted. Horseback riding is permitted on designated trails from October 16 to April 14 and on weekdays only from April 15 through October 15.*

needed rest stops in an annual journey that will take them as far north as the Arctic Circle. As many as 600 to 700 of the southbound migrants will winter over in these same protected waters from February to May. Here they walk the shoreline, feeding, resting and looking for small food-processing stones to swallow.

To protect the habitat of the black brant and other migrating and wintering waterfowl, the United States government established the Dungeness National Wildlife Refuge in 1915. The refuge is now managed by staff of the U.S. Fish and Wildlife Service's Nisqually National Wildlife Refuge Complex. Today, the spit of the 631-acre refuge is one of the region's last remaining stretches of natural beach in public ownership.

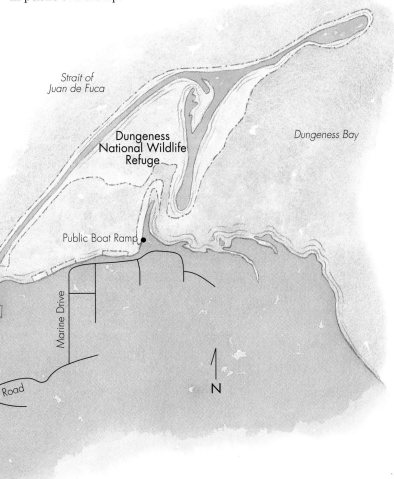

# BIG BEAVER CREEK
# RESEARCH NATURAL AREA

Roughly 10,000 to 12,000 years ago, the crenelated peaks of the North Cascade Mountains lay blanketed by a massive sheet of glacial ice. As the glaciers gradually withdrew, they left behind a legacy of cold alpine lakes, deeply furrowed moraines and broad floodplains underlain by glacial till. Plant communities were quick to colonize the isolated slopes and valleys of this newly revealed world.

In exactly this way, the breathtaking scenery and varied features of the Big Beaver Creek Research Natural Area (RNA) took shape. Spanning the floodplain and lower sideslopes of Big Beaver Creek in eastern Whatcom County, the RNA contains a mosaic of 28 types of identifiable plant communities. Here, botanists have identified 368 plant species belonging to 63 families—a tally that accounts for about 21 percent of the total number of taxa for the entire North Cascades ecosystem. Even to the untrained eye, the diversity of plants is astonishing—from stands of lodgepole pine to sphagnum-filled bogs.

Flowing through this exceptionally verdant garden is Big Beaver Creek, a major tributary that once entered the Skagit River from the west. Water from this and neighboring valleys now drains into Ross Lake, a massive hydroelectric and flood control reservoir currently maintained by Seattle City Light. Other smaller tributaries traverse the region, interconnecting numerous small, shallow ponds.

Created by glacial scour and the many beaver dams, from which Big Beaver Creek draws its name, the clear, oxygen-rich ponds and their feeder streams support a handful of salmonid fish species. Non-native cutthroat trout were introduced in the valley in 1916. Rainbow trout, native to the upper Skagit River, invade the valley stream system each summer, presumably to feed after the spawning season. Adult Dolly Varden char move in to spawn in September and October. Both feeding and spawning fish return to the Ross reservoir by late autumn.

The valley's cool, moist conditions also nurture an array of amphibians, including the Pacific tree frog, red-legged frog and western toad. North America's largest salamander, the Pacific giant salamander, and the strangely atavistic tailed frog are thought to exist here but have not been observed.

*Few Northwest natives can mistake the deeply furrowed bark of the Douglas-fir. This huge evergreen impressed the members of Captain Vancouver's expedition to the Northwest in 1792; they had never before seen such coniferous giants.*
*(Keith Lazelle)*

*The fisher leads a secretive life in Washington's old-growth forests.*

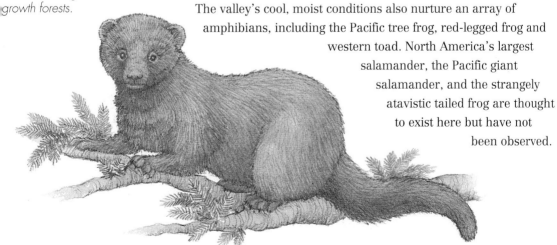

At least 69 species of breeding birds have been documented. Rare and sensitive species including the common loon, wood duck, harlequin duck, golden eagle, bald eagle and gray owl are frequently sighted. These birds are seen either in the valley or along Ross Lake, just off the mouth of Big Beaver Creek. Wolverine, black bear and fisher, currently listed as a sensitive species in Washington state, move quietly among the trees.

Big Beaver Valley is currently part of the North Cascades grizzly bear ecosystem, being studied as part of the recovery program for this endangered species. A small but expanding population of wolves has been observed nearby.

Steps to protect the lands surrounding the 3,142-acre RNA were first taken almost 100 years ago, when a presidential proclamation created the Washington Forest Reserve. In 1924, these lands became the Mount Baker National Forest, which in turn became North Cascades National Park, Ross Lake National Recreation Area and the Lake Chelan National Recreation Area. Roughly an eighth of the RNA's acreage falls within North Cascades National Park; the remainder is within the Ross Lake National Recreation Area. Along the RNA's longitudinal boundary is the Stephen Mather Wilderness, created by Congress in 1988. The RNA is managed by National Park Service staff headquartered at the North Cascades National Park office in Sedro Woolley.

*Pure and abundant fresh water from Big Beaver Creek nurtures this kaleidoscopic arrangement of maidenhair fern fronds.*
(Keith Lazelle)

*Stalks of red columbine speckle the banks. Their hues are a handsome contrast to this verdant green naturescape.*

(Keith Lazelle)

**Directions:** No roads lead directly to the RNA. It can be reached only by the Ross Dam Trailhead, a 6.8-mile foot/ horse trail from Milepost 134 on State Route 20 or by boat from Ross Dam or the Hozomeen area at the international boundary with Canada (at the north end of Ross Lake).

**Visitor access:** Camp only in designated campgrounds. Overnight visitors must obtain a backcountry permit from the Wilderness District Office at Marblemount.

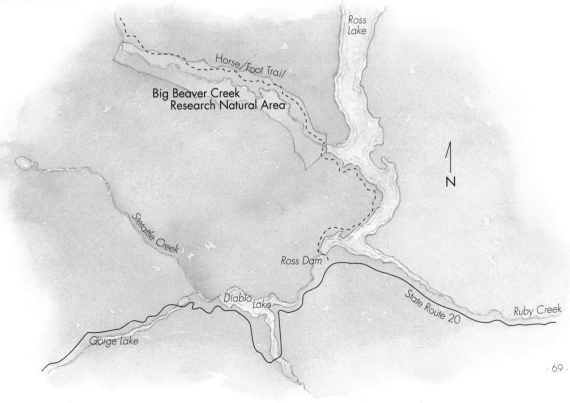

# ADDITIONAL PRESERVES
## — NOT OPEN FOR PUBLIC VISITATION —

### ISLANDS

"People like to save islands—particularly nice natural islands in very scenic places," The Nature Conservancy's Washington director, Elliot Marks, told readers of *Pacific Northwest Magazine* in 1986. Two years earlier, the Conservancy had mounted its campaign to save Pierce Island from development, bringing in donations from businesses, environmental groups and individuals interested in preserving wild islands.

In its 30-year history, the Washington Chapter of the Conservancy has put people's love of islands to good use. The Washington Chapter acquired its first island preserve on Waldron Island in 1972. Since then, five other locales in the San Juan Islands (including a second Waldron Island preserve) have been added to the Conservancy's roster of protected places. Given the sensitive nature of island ecosystems, many of these preserves are only open to participants of approved research and education projects.

San Juan County and its neighbor to the south, Island County, are among the fastest-growing counties in the state. For the last 20 years, real estate sales and development in the San Juans have been booming. As the market continues to spiral, entire inhabitable islands are seldom available. Those parcels of land that appear on the market command premium prices. With the demand for isolated getaway homes, the few significant remaining natural areas are rapidly disappearing.

Only by acquiring undisturbed portions of islands and, where possible, entire islands, has the Conservancy been successful in setting aside habitat for the tufted puffin, bald eagle and other native animals and plants that are less tolerant of human activity.

The Conservancy's three-acre Goose Island Preserve, acquired in 1975, contains a small but excellent example of dry-site open grassland vegetation unique to the San Juans. It is also home to a colony of glaucous-winged gulls and nesting black oystercatchers. Goose Island also provides feeding and resting habitat for harlequin ducks, black turnstones, marbled murrelets, pigeon guillemots, northern phalarope and tufted puffins.

Acquired at the same time as Goose Island, the Deadman Island Preserve is a two-acre geologist's dream. This small spot of land in Cattle Pass is an exposed submarine fan deposit, possibly created millions of years ago during a massive, violent movement of the earth's crust. Today Deadman's rocks, reefs and tidepools host a fascinating array of marine plants and animals. Like its neighbor, Goose Island, Deadman is managed solely for research and educational purposes in cooperation with the University of Washington's Friday Harbor Marine Laboratories.

The 15-acre Sentinel Island Preserve was the last island in the San Juans to be homesteaded; its settlers, the Burn family, never logged the land or allowed it to be extensively grazed. Flowers predominate on the south-facing portion of the island, and a forest of Douglas-fir, grand fir, western hemlock, Pacific madrone, Oregon white oak and Douglas maple cloaks the remainder. Sentinel Island and Yellow Island (described earlier in this book) were both acquired as part of the Conservancy's highly successful Islands of Life fundraising campaign of 1979-80. The initial campaign raised $425,000 for purchasing land, and subsequent fundraising enabled the Conservancy to establish a $200,000 endowment for the management of the two islands.

*The tufted puffin—with its distinctive white face, prominent orange-red bill and wispy crown of feathers—nests in isolated parts of Washington's coastal waters.*
*(Art Wolfe)*

# GRASSLANDS

When first settled by European-American pioneers in the late 19th century, the 14-million-acre Columbia Basin was covered with an intricate mosaic of native shrubs and perennial bunchgrasses. Settlement wrought profound changes to the Basin's ecosystems. The region's deep soils were plowed and planted, displacing the natural systems. Later, large-scale irrigation projects enabled the most arid lands to be farmed. Non-arable land was grazed by cattle and sheep.

Unlike some native ecosystems, the Basin's grasslands do not often revert to native plant types if grazing or farming ceases on a site. In many instances, the introduction of alien plants—aggressive, fast-growing exotic species such as cheat grass and Kentucky bluegrass—has caused irreversible change.

Of the 39 types of plant communities native to the Columbia Basin few representative examples are known to remain in good condition. Good examples of 14 grassland communities can no longer be located and may be completely eliminated in our state. As the few relatively pristine sites diminish, the number of animals and plants that depend on native grassland habitats—including threatened species like the pygmy rabbit and ferruginous hawk, the Columbia milkvetch and Washington polemonium—also decrease.

In efforts to preserve the state's splendid grassland heritage, The Nature Conservancy continues to identify and acquire the best

Listed as a sensitive species in Washington, the Piper's daisy is one of many rare grassland flowers.
(Mark Sheehan)

remaining grassland examples. Today, the Washington Chapter provides long-term stewardship for 800 acres of native grassland, some of the finest-quality examples that remain.

Some of the Conservancy's grassland preserves, such as the 25-acre Eugene C. Phillips Memorial Preserve, are small fragments of original ecosystems. The Washington Chapter of the Conservancy acquired this land in 1980 as a gift from the descendants of Eugene C. Phillips. The area hosts the rare Piper's daisy, listed as a sensitive species in Washington. One hundred of these small, flowering survivors can be found overlooking wheat fields and range land.

A much larger grassland is protected within the Malott Flats Preserve. One of the finest grasslands remaining in Eastern Washington, it hosts plant communities dominated by Idaho fescue, bluebunch wheatgrass and antelope bitterbrush. Bitterbrush, a greenish shrub that stands as tall as six feet, is a favored browse for both white-tailed and mule deer. Between 1982-89, the Conservancy acquired most of the preserve's 339 acres. Today, the Conservancy retains ownership of 40 acres while the remainder is managed by the DNR preserve system.

*Bunchgrass communities are extremely fragile. Without protection, we could lose rare grassland habitats, like this one at Malott Flats Preserve. (Harold E. Malde)*

## WETLANDS

Wetlands provide essential feeding, nesting, brooding and cover habitat for many species of birds, fish, reptiles, invertebrates and mammals. They are nurseries for juvenile fish and other small organisms, anchors against shoreline erosion, filters for particles and pollutants and barriers to flooding. At least a third of Washington's threatened and endangered species rely on natural wetlands for their survival.

Once considered worthless swamps, these vital habitats have been destroyed by dredging, draining and diking. The pace of wetland destruction continues at an alarming rate. Studies indicate that more

*Following the widespread loss of its sagebrush habitat, the threatened pygmy rabbit has nearly disappeared from Washington.*

*Salt marshes are of utmost importance to flocks of snow geese, which winter along the western edge of Washington's Puget Sound. Marsh plants provide the nourishment that the geese need to complete their long flights to and from Siberian breeding grounds.*
(Art Wolfe)

than half of our nation's wetlands have been converted to other uses, including agricultural, industrial and residential development.

Today, more than half of Washington's original saltwater marshes have been destroyed or seriously altered. Of the wetlands that remain, many have been degraded by chemical pollution, inadequate waste treatment, sedimentation from logging and road construction and diversion of water for agriculture. Still other wetlands that appear undisturbed have been invaded by alien plant species that aggressively displace native species.

In 1986, the Washington Chapter of the Conservancy initiated a campaign to permanently protect 10 of the state's highest-quality wetland areas. These preserves now serve as living museums and outdoor laboratories, safeguarding rare and endangered plant and animal species and providing comparative baseline information for restoring degraded areas.

The Nature Conservancy co-owns the 1,700-acre Bone River Estuary Natural Area Preserve with the DNR. Located on Willapa Bay in Pacific County, the Bone River Estuary and its surroundings form one of the three high-quality estuarine ecosystems that remain on Washington's outer coast.

The Bone River Preserve rolls gently toward the water, with a few short, steep pitches between bottomland and conifer forest. Viewed from afar, its marshes look like meadows. Green in summer and golden-brown through fall, tufted hairgrass ordinarily dominates much of the higher marsh areas. It is the tallest plant of the salt marsh, dwarfing its companion, the strawberry-like Pacific silverweed. At low tide, the barren mudflats beyond these estuarine meadows become important foraging grounds for migrating waterfowl and shorebirds.

South of the Bone River Preserve, The Nature Conservancy owns a portion of the Niawiakum River Estuary Natural Area Preserve. The Conservancy assisted with acquisition efforts for most of the 800-acre preserve, most of which is owned by the DNR.

A 21.5-acre, triangular-shaped parcel in Grays Harbor County, the Humptulips River Delta Preserve was donated to the Conservancy in 1988. The site includes two superb examples of native salt marsh types, both of statewide ecological significance, with a contiguous brackish water tideland.

At first glance, the Moxee Bog Preserve appears far from exceptional. Yet this 10-acre site in Yakima County is a geologic anomaly—a relic of the last ice age that provides habitat for species of organisms that have been absent from the surrounding area for thousands of years. One such biological holdout is the silver-bordered bog fritillary, a small orange and black butterfly, currently listed by the state as a sensitive species. Scientists believe that the original habitat of the silver-bordered bog fritillary and its food source, a species of purple bog violet, dwindled with the retreat of the glaciers, leaving only small pockets, like Moxee Bog, where the larvae of the butterfly can feed.

Acquired in 1966, the bog lies amid dry, sagebrush-covered hills and is fed by a series of cold-water springs. A floating mat of vegetation covering the bog is nearly two feet thick.

*The Bone River's lush, green estuary is a haven and feeding ground for a wide variety of wildlife.*
*(Sunny Walter)*

***Overleaf**: Great blue herons stalk the mud flats of Willapa Bay at day's end.*
*(Keith Lazelle)*

*"Conservation is sometimes perceived as stopping everything cold. … The choice is not between wild places or people. Rather, it is between a rich or an impoverished existence."*

—Thomas Lovejoy

# THE FUTURE OF BIODIVERSITY

*by Elliot Marks, Washington Director of The Nature Conservancy*

Safeguarding natural diversity is urgent and complex. Since 1951, land acquisition has been The Nature Conservancy's primary tactic in this effort. However, to effectively protect the state's biological diversity, we cannot rely merely on our own acquisition efforts or the shifting sands of governmental regulation.

An effective agenda for the future must address several key issues if we are to slow the current rate of plant and animal extinction—now estimated at between three and 25 species each day—and conserve more than the finite havens for nature that our preserves represent.

## CONSERVING ECOSYSTEMS

If our preserves are regarded as lifeboats of biodiversity, we need to conserve some battleships as well. Internationally, the Conservancy has committed itself to a wide variety of landscape-sized projects. Strategies for these projects will focus on a common theme: working with local communities to ensure the maintenance of environmental quality and species diversity while promoting truly sustainable economic development.

The notion that communities must choose between jobs and the environment is a false one. A healthy, sustainable economy and a healthy environment are mutually dependent. Citizens want economic growth, but not at the expense of our environment. The Conservancy can help communities reach this goal by providing some of the tools and support necessary for making sound resource-management decisions. While this community support includes the Conservancy's traditional land-acquisition approach, most of the lands within these areas will be owned or managed by other groups or individuals.

*Swift-flowing waters and numerous snags are among the many positive indicators of the Big Beaver Creek Research Natural Area's relatively undisturbed condition.*

*(Keith Lazelle)*

The pygmy owl frequents the edges of open coniferous forests or mixed woodlands. It nests in woodpecker holes.
(Keith Lazelle)

## PROMOTING STEWARDSHIP

We must fulfill our promise to care for the lands that we own. And we hope to influence others to carefully manage their lands. Fulfilling this promise is more complex than simply preserving or restoring to natural conditions the habitats we control. We need to focus our attention on managing the biological "elements"—the rare plants, animals and ecosystems—found on our preserves.

The Conservancy works to achieve model stewardship by applying our knowledge of natural systems to each preserve in the state. As we progress, we strive to learn more about the needs of and intricate relationships between species and natural systems.

For example, to make good management decisions about an endangered plant and its habitat we must first identify the conditions that both require to survive. Does the plant rely on certain insects for pollination? Does it require a special water regime provided by seasonal floods or droughts? Does it depend on occasional fires to maintain its population? What will happen to its water supply if surrounding land is converted to another use?

To answer these complex questions regarding the individual elements of our preserves, we need to sponsor more primary research. Only then will we be able to appropriately manage the important natural features on our preserves in the coming years.

In addition to managing land, plants and animals, our stewardship efforts must also include managing people. As the state's natural areas dwindle, our preserves will become increasingly attractive to the public. Even today our staff must weigh the advantages of publicizing certain places to help fund their protection against the drawbacks of having people "love" certain resources to death.

# SHAPING PUBLIC LAND-MANAGEMENT GOALS

About 40 percent of Washington's landscape is publicly owned. The Washington Chapter has worked hard to secure commitments for land protection and management from the appropriate state and federal agencies. In addition to efforts with state and national legislative bodies, the local chapter of the Conservancy has constructed a Public Lands Protection Program and has utilized the inventory and informational functions of the state's Natural Heritage Program.

In the past, most natural resource agencies have largely focused on specific "products," such as ducks, salmon, deer, timber, grass and water. While all of these "commodities" are still needed from public lands, managers are now being confronted with other public concerns, including incorporating the preservation of biodiversity into their land-management goals.

An ongoing challenge to the Washington Chapter is to encourage and help facilitate the evolution of Washington's natural resource agencies. We must continue to work cooperatively with these agencies as they redefine their mission. One important way the Washington Chapter has and will continue to promote management for biodiversity is to help provide private financial resources and constituency support.

Public agencies respond more quickly to a positive, problem-solving approach than to shrill criticism and rebukes. The Conservancy must position itself as a primary resource for conservation management and restoration ecology. This is especially important as the movement toward privatization of governmental functions gains momentum.

*A state-threatened species, the Oregon checker-mallow is found on only a few sites in Washington, including areas protected by The Nature Conservancy.*
*(Nature Conservancy file)*

## BUILDING NEW COALITIONS AND PARTNERSHIPS

Learning to live in harmony with natural systems will be the greatest challenge of the post-wilderness conservation era. Merely enjoying the mining of our natural resources has been sufficient to date, but the party is quickly coming to an end.

In economic terms, we've been living off our biological capital in the mistaken belief that our resources are infinite. We now understand that there are real limits to what the natural systems of our planet can provide and the wastes they can absorb. We need to learn to live off the interest, not the capital. Our economic balance sheets must reflect both negative impacts to natural resources and positive contributions to ecosystems.

Our greatest successes in Washington have come from a conscious effort to build coalitions and seek mutual understanding and consensus. In recent years, we have enjoyed outstanding results with this approach to resolving disputes over natural resources. Admittedly, the number of issues that can be settled in this way is limited. Yet it's encouraging to see parties turn to mediation as an alternative to confrontation to resolve resource disputes.

*Endangered sandhill cranes no longer nest in numbers in Washington. However, both greater and lesser sandhills continue to stop over during spring and fall migrations.*

Few mammals are as playful or well suited to waterfront life as the river otter, found on several Conservancy wetland preserves in the state. (Joel Rogers)

In the coming years, our stature and experience should enable us to act as peacemakers in many resource disputes. We have established open lines of communication with nearly all parties representing key economic interests. Consequently, we are well positioned as facilitators in these conflicts and can play an important part in their outcome.

Another critical need is to expand the diversity of the conservation movement, which is now largely composed of well-educated, middle class people. Environmental degradation has had a disproportionate impact on poor people throughout the world. While numerous polls have shown that 75 percent of our state's population considers itself environmentally concerned, conservation organizations, including the Washington Chapter, need to expand their membership to include different economic groups.

# UNDERSTANDING RESTORATION ECOLOGY

Although the science of restoration ecology is relatively new, it's certain to become a dominant concern in the next century. The Washington Chapter has an opportunity and, I think, an obligation to be a leader in helping to heal the Earth. Efforts to increase public and private funding for habitat restoration will generate important new opportunities to implement recovery plans for important species and ecosystems.

Working with the conviction that nature knows best, we can try to restore and improve damaged areas by mimicking the native systems we have protected on our preserves. In this respect, our preserves will serve as reservoirs of the natural perfection that evolved over millions of years.

The Washington Chapter of The Nature Conservancy can be proud of what it has accomplished. Its positive, scientific and highly focused approach has made a difference and will leave an unparalleled legacy for our children.

The eastern kingbird, a member of the flycatcher family, is found on several Conservancy preserves in Eastern Washington.
(Sunny Walter)

Moon and madrone complete a sunset portrait of Washington's wildlands.
(Keith Lazelle)

# OTHER AGENCIES & ORGANIZATIONS

The following agencies and organizations play important roles in protecting natural areas in our state for ecological, scientific and educational purposes. For more information, contact these offices:

National Park Service
Chief, Division of Lands
Pacific Northwest Region
83 S. King St., Suite 212
Seattle, WA 98104-2887

U.S. Bureau of Land Management
Border Resource Area
East 4217 Main Ave.
Spokane, WA 99202

U.S. Bureau of Land Management
Wenatchee Resource Area
1133 N. Western Ave.
Wenatchee, WA 98801

U.S. Fish & Wildlife Service
Regional Supervisor
Division of Realty
911 N.E. 11th Ave.
Portland, OR 97232-4181

U.S. Forest Service
Director of Lands & Minerals
Pacific Northwest Region
333 S.W. First St.
P.O. Box 3623-97208
Portland, OR 97208

Washington Department of Natural Resources
Natural Heritage Program Manager
P.O. Box 47047
Olympia, WA 98504-7047

Washington Department of Wildlife
Assistant Director
Land Resources Division
600 Capitol Way N.
Olympia, WA 98501-1091

Washington State Parks & Recreation Commission
Chief, Site Planning & Acquisition
7150 Cleanwater Lane
P.O. Box 42650
Olympia, WA 98504-2650

# THE NATURE CONSERVANCY

The Nature Conservancy is an international, private, non-profit conservation organization dedicated to preserving plants, animals and ecosystems that represent the diversity of life on Earth by protecting the lands and waters they need to survive. Since 1951, The Nature Conservancy and its members have safeguarded more than 6.3 million acres of our finest natural lands and the diversity of life they shelter—from lush wetlands and dense forests to dry grasslands and arid deserts. By acquiring ecologically significant lands through purchase or donation, the Conservancy now owns and manages more than 1,300 preserves, the largest system of private nature sanctuaries in the world.

Built on a strong scientific foundation, the Conservancy works to :

- IDENTIFY the most important natural areas that remain
- PROTECT the lands through direct purchase, gift, conservation easement or voluntary registration
- MANAGE preserves for long-term conservation
- INFORM people about the importance of protecting natural lands.

In Washington, the Conservancy has protected native species and ecosystems on more than 20,000 acres across the state, including 26 preserves owned and managed by the Washington Chapter.

To find out how you can support The Nature Conservancy or become a member, please contact:

> The Nature Conservancy
> Washington Chapter
> 217 Pine Street, Suite 1100
> Seattle, Washington 98101
> (206) 343-4344

Nature Conservancy preserves
open for visitation
(see Table of Contents)

Other preserve areas featured
in book (see Table of Contents)

Other Nature Conservancy
preserves

Other preserves protected with
Nature Conservancy assistance

Since its founding in 1961, The Nature Conservancy's Washington Chapter has purchased and protected thousands of acres of ecologically important lands in the state. The Conservancy currently owns and manages 26 nature preserves in Washington, part of the largest system of private nature sanctuaries in the world. The Conservancy has also assisted several public agencies with acquisition of many important natural areas at the agencies' request. The following list identifies many of these preserves and the rare natural features they protect for future generations.

## KEY OF AGENCIES & ORGANIZATIONS:

| | |
|---|---|
| COV | City of Vancouver |
| CWU | Central Washington University |
| DNR | Washington Department of Natural Resources |
| ESD | Edmonds School District |
| NPS | National Park Service |
| SCL | Seattle City Light |
| SCP | Spokane County Parks |
| TNC | The Nature Conservancy |
| USFS | U.S. Forest Service |
| WDW | Washington Department of Wildlife |
| WPR | Washington Parks and Recreation |
| WWU | Western Washington University |

| PRESERVE | MANAGER | PROTECTED FEATURES |
|---|---|---|
| Anderson Lake | WPR | Woodland |
| Badger Gulch | DNR | Grassland, rare plants |
| Bald Hill | DNR | Forest, grassland, rare plants |
| Barker Mountain | TNC | Forest, grassland |
| Birch Bay/Blackwood | WPR | Wetland |
| Bone River Estuary | TNC/DNR | Wetland |
| Boots Satterlee | TNC | Wetland |
| Burnt Bridge Creek Canyon | COV | Woodland, wetland |
| Carlisle Bog | DNR | Wetland, rare plant & animal |
| Castle Rock | DNR/WPR | Grassland |
| Chase Lake Bog | ESD | Bog |
| Chuckanut Island | TNC | Rare animal |
| Cypress Highlands | DNR | Grassland, forest |
| Dabob Bay | TNC/DNR | Wetland, grassland |
| Deadman Island | TNC | Bird breeding habitat |
| Deering Wildflower Acres | WWU | Forest |
| Dishman Hills | TNC/DNR | Forest, grassland |
| Engelhorn Pond | CWU | Woodland, pond |
| Florence Lake | WDW | Rare animal |
| Foulweather Bluff | TNC | Wetland, forest |
| Goose Island | TNC | Bird breeding habitat |
| Humptulips River Delta | TNC | Wetland |
| Kings Lake Bog | DNR | Wetland, rare animal |
| Lake Louise | WWU | Pond |
| Larkspur Meadows | DNR | Rare plants |
| Lake Quinault Acreage | NPS | Forest |
| Robert W. Little | TNC | Rare animal |
| Little Spokane River | SCP | Riparian habitat |
| Magnuson Butte | TNC | Grassland |
| Malott Flats | TNC/DNR | Grassland |
| Methow Rapids | DNR | Grassland |
| Mima Mounds | DNR | Grassland, rare plant |
| Moxee Bog | TNC | Wetland, rare animal |
| Niawiakum River Estuary | TNC/DNR | Wetland |
| Noisy Creek | USFS | Forest |
| North Bay | DNR | Wetland, rare animal |
| Eugene C. Phillips Memorial | TNC | Grassland, rare plant |
| Pierce Island | TNC | Forest, rare plants & animals |
| Point of Arches | NPS | Coastal forest |
| Protection Island | WDW | Bird breeding habitat |
| Rasar State Park | WPR | Forest |
| Ritzville Shrub Steppe | TNC | Grassland, vernal ponds |
| Rose Creek | TNC | Plant community |
| Sauk Mountain | WPR | Rare animal |
| Seaton Canyon | TNC | Grassland |
| Sentinel Island | TNC | Bird & marine life habitat |
| Skagit River Bald Eagle Natural Area | TNC/WDW/DNR USFS/WPR/SCL | Rare animal |
| Skookum Inlet | DNR | Wetland |
| Snoqualmie Bog | DNR | Wetland, rare animal |
| Waldron Island | TNC | Woodland, bird habitat |
| Willapa Divide | DNR | Forest |
| Yellow Island | TNC | Grassland |

PRODUCTION NOTES

Preserving Washington Wildlands *was
produced on a Macintosh desktop
publishing system using PageMaker
software.*

*The text font is Linotype Centennial;
captions are set in Futura.*

*Color separations of photographs and
illustrations were traditionally scanned.*

*Paper stock is Warren Lustro Gloss
Recycled 100# text with matching
100# cover. It is made of at least
10% post-consumer waste with total
recycled fiber content of at least 50%.*